The Real Vegetarian Cookbook

Super Simple Vegetarian Recipes for Every Day including Bonus: 28 Days Vegetarian Weight Loss Challenge

[1st Edition]

Sarah Rose Elridge

This book is intended to be informative and helpful and contains the opinions and ideas of the author. The author intends to teach in an entertaining manner. Some recipes may not suit all readers. Use this book and implement the guides and recipes at your own will, taking responsibility and risk where it falls. This work with all its contents, does not guarantee correctness, completion, quality or correctness of the provided information. Misinformation or misprints cannot be completely eliminated.

According to the Vegetarian Society, "vegetarians and vegans don't eat products or by-products of slaughter. They don't eat any foods which have been made using processing aids from slaughter".

A vegetarian's diet can include:

- Vegetables and fruits (no exceptions)
- Grains and foods made from grains (rice, buckwheat, barley, wheat, oats, corn, etc.)
- Pulses (beans, peas, soy, chickpeas, lentils, etc.)
- Nuts (walnuts, Brazilian nuts, pecans, pea nuts, pistachios, almonds, etc.)
- Seeds (quinoa, chia, hemp, sesame, flax, pumpkin seeds, sunflower seeds, etc.)
- Eggs (preferably free-range and organic)
- Dairy products (milk, cheese, yogurt, sour cream, crème fraiche, etc.)
- Honey

A vegetarian's diet cannot include:

- Meat or poultry (irrespective of source)
- Fish or seafood (irrespective of source)

- Insects (often found as hidden ingredients)
- Animal rennet or gelatine
- Fat from animals or animal stock

Vegetarianism is a very straightforward concept. Vegetarians change their eating habits based on ethical, environmental, and/or health concerns. Going veggie is one of the easiest and most efficient ways to decrease your environmental footprint as well as save the lives of hundreds of animals. In addition, being vegetarian allows you to lead a healthier lifestyle, which entails plenty of whole grains, fresh vegetables and fruit.

For many years, scientists have studied vegetarianism to discover potential nutritional deficiencies. However, the results have come to confirm quite the contrary: a vegetarian, or meet-free, diet comes with multiple health benefits. Not only is a vegetarian diet nutritionally sufficient, but it is also the most effective way to minimise the risk of developing chronic illnesses. But what does a health

People of all ages can embrace a vegetarian diet if they are eating a healthy meet-free diet. Keyword is healthy. Being a vegetarian is more than just not eating products or by-products of slaughter. Being a vegetarian is about being healthier. The healthier we remain on the long term, the more rewarding our lives and the higher the quality of our living.

Eating soda, cheese pizza, and candy is, technically, eating meet-free. It may satisfy an environmental or ethical vegetarian, but it will certainly not contribute to your health in the long term. Therefore, being meet-free diet is not enough. You must eat an appropriately planned vegetarian diet that follows the recommended guidelines for weight control, fat consumption, and nutrition.

Technically, veganism is a form of vegetarianism where you eliminate animal-derived products from your vegetarian diet. While a vegetarian can eat dairy products, honey, and eggs, a vegan cannot. The main reasoning behind veganism is ethical and environmental.

Thus, hens that produce eggs are still sacrificed and are also often kept in miserable conditions, unable to move. Bees die to make additional honey because when we consume honey, we are essentially consuming their food. Therefore, more bees need to die for us to eat honey. Similar reasoning stands behind not consuming milk.

However, vegetarians often try to get their eggs, dairy products, and honey from free-range or organic eggs exclusively. They often buy milk from sustainable, cruelty-free farms, and try to buy honey that is produced reasonably.

By simply eliminating meat from your diet, you are already a conscientious, ethical eater. However, the quality of the meet-free foods you eat is extremely important. There are several healthy vegetarian principles that you must keep in mind when you add foods to your shopping cart:

1. **Include as many foods as you can from all food categories in your vegetarian diet!** You may not like milk, but that is no reason to exclude all dairy products. There must be one yogurt or cheese that satisfies your taste buds. The same applies for grains, fruits, nuts and seeds, or pulses.

2. **Substitute saturated and trans fats with healthy fats!** Healthy fats come from extra-virgin olive oil, other minimally processed vegetable oils, as well as nuts and seeds, or avocados.

3. **Keep track of calories!** Nuts and seeds are amazing but it's very easy to abuse them calorie-wise. The same applies for many vegetarian foods. They are extremely nutritious but also calorie rich. So, count calories and portion control. Use an app to do the job for you. All you need to do is to enter everything you eat.

4. **Read food labels!** It is amazing if you can cook every day and minimize the use of processed foods, but the truth is

not many people do it. So, they opt for processed foods. However, not all processed foods have been created made equal. Check labels so you stay away from added sugar, all sorts of additives, and ingredients you can't read. If you must choose some processed foods, choose the healthiest possible version

5. ***Track nutrition!*** As a vegetarian, you must pay attention to certain nutrients. These nutrients include fats and omegas, vitamin B12, calcium, iodine, iron, protein, vitamin D, and zinc. Use an online app to track everything and adjust diet accordingly.

Reading labels is very important, not only from a health perspective, but also from a vegetarian perspective. There are many hidden ingredients in processed foods, including animal rennet or gelatine, animal fat, or animal stock. Gummy sweets are a good example as they contain gelatine.

From a definition perspective, people who do not consume poultry, meat, or seafood are called vegetarians. However, in time, different dietary patterns have led to the development of certain varieties of vegetarians, including:

1. **Total vegetarians or vegans:** Vegans don't eat meat, seafood, or poultry, as well as any animal-derived products, including dairy, eggs, and honey.

2. **Ovo-lacto vegetarians:** Ovo-lacto vegetarians are your typical vegetarians that do not eat meat, seafood, or poultry, but eat dairy products and eggs.

3. **Lacto vegetarians:** Lactovegetarians are vegetarians that eat dairy products, but do not eat eggs, meat, fish, or poultry.

4. **Ovo-vegetarians:** Ovo-vegetarians are vegetarians that eat eggs, but do not eat fish, meat, poultry, or dairy products.

5. **Pesco-vegetarians or pescatarians:** Pescatarians are partial vegetarians that not do not eat meat or poultry but eat fish.

6. **Pollo-vegetarians:** Pollo-vegetarians are partial vegetarians that do not eat meat or fish but eat poultry.

Prep Time: 5 minutes | Cook time: 10 minutes | Serves: 2

Nutrition per 1 serving: Calories: 451 | Carbs: 2 g | Fibres: 0 g | Fat: 36 g | Protein: 26 g

Ingredients:

◇ 5 egg whites (large, free-range)

◇ 3 egg yolks (large, free-range)

◇ 2 tbsps. organic butter (unsalted)

◇ Salt and pepper to taste

For serving:

◇ Finely chopped chives, or

◇ Finelychopped parsley

Preparation:

1. Use a hand whisk to mix the yolks until the mixture becomes pale. Set aside.

2. Start whisking the egg whites until they form a white, peaky foam and triple in volume. Use an electric mixer to get quicker results.

3. Use a spatula to fold the egg yolks into the egg whites. Make sure to incorporate the egg yolks perfectly without overmixing.

4. Place a frying pan of medium size on moderate heat. Drop half of the butter and allow to melt. Spread the eggs onto the pan as uniformly as you can. Reduce the heat and give the eggs 5 minutes to cook on low.

5. Lift the omelette with a spatula and add the rest of the butter onto the pan. Cover with a lid and cook for 6 more minutes. The omelette is done when the top (including the centre) has set.

6. Remove the lid and season the omelette to taste. Fold and divide in two portions. Plate the omelette and sprinkle with the green garnish of choice. Enjoy!

Prep Time: 10 minutes | Cook time: 5 minutes | Serves: 1

Nutrition per 1 serving: Calories: 548 | Carbs: 26 g | Fibres: 7 g | Fat: 38 g | Protein: 30 g

Ingredients:

- ◇ ½ tbsp. unsalted butter
- ◇ 2 free-range eggs
- ◇ 40 g onion (cooked)
- ◇ 25 g bell pepper (cooked)
- ◇ 25 g cheddar cheese (grated)
- ◇ 1 tbsp. parmesan cheese (grated)
- ◇ 40 g black beans (from can)
- ◇ 3 slices avocado
- ◇ Salt to taste

Preparation:

1. In a bowl, mix eggs and parmesan cheese into a homogenous mixture. Salt to taste. Set aside.

2. Melt the butter over moderate-low heat in a medium-sized pan. Spread the egg and parmesan mixture onto the pan. Cook until almost set. In the centre of the cheese omelette, add the cheddar cheese, the cooked bell pepper and onions, and the black beans.

3. Place a lid over the pan. Cook for 3 minutes. Arrange the three avocado slices over the veggies. Remove the pan from heat and plate the omelette.

4. Fold the omelette like you would fold a burrito and enjoy!

Prep Time: 2 minutes | Cook time: 0 minutes| Serves: 1

Nutrition per 1 serving: Calories: 407 | Carbs: 38.4 g | Fibres: 8.7 g | Fat: 22.8 g | Protein: 12.5 g

Ingredients:

◇ 200 ml plain Greek yogurt

◇ 50 g raspberries

◇ 50g blueberries

◇ 50g strawberries

◇ 30 g vegetarian granola

◇ cinnamon (optional)

Preparation:

1 Place ½ of the yogurt in a mason jar. Add half of the granola. Add the half of the berries. Repeat. Top with cinnamon powder to taste!

2 Enjoy!

Prep Time: 5 minutes | Cook time: 0 minutes | Serves: 1

Nutrition per 1 serving: Calories: 444 | Carbs: 56 g | Fibres: 10 g | Fat: 20 g | Protein: 15 g

Ingredients:

◇ 50 g instant oatmeal

◇ Hot water

◇ 1 banana (sliced)

◇ 35 g nuts of choice

◇ Cinnamon powder to taste (optional)

◇ Salt to taste (optional)

Preparation:

1 Add the instant oatmeal in a see-through jar or bowl. Add the cinnamon powder and salt to taste (optional). Pour hot water (or milk) as per package instructions. Stir. Set aside for 2 minutes.

2 Place the banana slices and nuts in the oatmeal mixture and give it a quick mix. Enjoy!

Nutrition per 1 serving: Calories: 455 | Carbs: 1.7 g | Fibres: 0 g | Fat: 37.9 g | Protein: 25 g

Ingredients:

◇ 1 tbsp. olive oil

◇ 3 large free-range eggs

◇ Gouda cheese (1 slice)

◇ Salt and pepper to taste

For serving:

◇ Freshly chopped parsley or chives

Preparation:

1 Whisk the three eggs in a bowl until they form a frothy, homogenous mixture. Season to taste.

2 Add the olive oil to a pan and heat quickly on moderate heat. Pour the eggs. Move the pan to spread the eggs in a uniform layer. Give the omelette 1 minute to cook on moderate heat.

3 Lower heat on your stove. Let the eggs cook until they are almost set. Gently place the slice of gouda cheese in the centre. Fold the omelette. Cook for half a minute on each side.

GOUDA-FILLED BREAKFAST OMELETTE

Prep Time:15 minutes | Cook time: 15 minutes | Serves: 2

Nutrition per 2 servings: Calories: 909 | Carbs: | 2.2 g | Fibres: 14.4 g | Fat: 71.9 g | Protein: 38.9 g

Ingredients:

◇ Multigrain crispbread thins (4)

◇ 2 free range eggs (hardboiled)

◇ 50 g Brie cheese (cubed)

◇ 1 ripe avocado (California type, black skin)

◇ 50 g Blue Stilton cheese (cubed)

◇ 100g cherry tomatoes (halved)

◇ Italian herbs mix (optional)

◇ Olive oil spray (20 sprays)

◇ Salt and pepper to taste

Preparation:

1 Cut the avocado in half and remove the pit. Spoon out the flesh and slice finely. Place equally on plates. Add the halved cherry tomatoes.

2 Cut the hardboiled eggs to desired shape and size. Arrange them on plates next to the cherry tomatoes and avocado slices. Add the cubed brie and Stilton to the plates.

3 Spray the veggies and cheeses with olive oil. Sprinkle Italian seasonings on top. Season with salt and pepper! Serve with crispbread thins! Enjoy!

Prep Time: 5 minutes | Cook time: 5 minutes | Serves: 2

Nutrition per 2 servings: Calories: 680 | Carbs: 40 g | Fibres: 11.5 g | Fat: 44 g | Protein: 34 g

Ingredients:

◇ 2 bread slices (toasted)

◇ 1 avocado (California type, black skin)

◇ 2 slices mozzarella cheese

◇ 2 large free-range eggs

◇ 4 cherry tomatoes (finely sliced

◇ 1 tbsp. vegetable oil

◇ Salt and pepper to taste

Preparation:

1 Heat the oil in a frying pan. Crack the two eggs and cook to preference. Remove from pan onto a plate.

2 In a mortar, add the avocado flesh and use the pestle to mash it into a smooth paste. Season with salt and pepper to taste.

3 Spread the avocado mash on the toasted bread slices. Grab a slice of mozzarella and place it on top. Top each slice with one egg and season to preference. Enjoy!

Prep Time: 2 minutes | Cook time: 2 minutes | Serves: 2

Nutrition per 2 servings: Calories: 734 | Carbs: 78 g | Fibres: 10 g | Fat: 39 g | Protein: 24 g

Ingredients:

◇ 275g plain Greek yogurt
◇ 350 ml whole cow's milk (or milk of choice)
◇ 300 g frozen strawberry slices
◇ 1 frozen banana (previously sliced)
◇ Blender (for processing)

Preparation:

1 Add the yogurt and milk to a blender. Add the frozen strawberries and bananas. Blend to desired smoothness. Enjoy!

2 For a sweet flavour, stir in agave or maple syrup!

Prep Time: 2 minutes | Cook time: 2 minutes | Serves: 1

Nutrition per 1 serving: Calories: 495 | Carbs: 51 g | Fibres: 8 g | Fat: 24 g | Protein: 20 g

Ingredients:

- ◈ 160 ml milk, of your choice
- ◈ 1 ½ frozen bananas
- ◈ 35g plain oat
- ◈ 2 tbsps. 100% peanut butter
- ◈ 2 tsps. cocoa powder

Preparation:

1. Add all the ingredients to a blender and mix for 30 seconds. If needed, use a spatula to scrape any mixture down the sides. Mix for an additional 20-40 seconds.

2. Transfer the smoothie to a mason jar or an air-tight cup. Place in the fridge until ready to indulge! Enjoy!

Prep Time: 5 minutes | Cook time: 5 minutes | Serves: 1

Nutrition per 1 serving: Calories: 436 | Carbs: 2 g | Fibres: 0 g | Fat: 31 g | Protein: 33 g

Ingredients:

◈ 1 tbsp.olive oil

◈ Salt and pepper to taste

◈ 2 free-range eggs

◈ 4 shiitake mushrooms (sliced)

◈ 20g baby spinach leaves (chopped)

◈ 2 tbsps. grated cheddar cheese (coloured)

◈ Chopped scallions, chives, or parsley (for serving)

Preparation:

1 Whisk the eggs in a mixing bowl into a homogenous mixture. Add all remaining omelette ingredients except for the mushrooms and whisk to combine. Season to taste.

2 Heat the olive oil in a pan. Grab the mushrooms and add them to the shimmering oil. Fry for 2 minutes while stirring occasionally. Transfer the fried shiitake to the egg mixture bowl. Whisk to combine.

3 Add the eggs and shiitake mixture to the same pan. Set heat to moderate and cook for 1 minute. Lower heat and fry until the eggs are set. Plate the omelette and enjoy with fresh herb of choice. Enjoy!

Prep Time: 5 minutes | Cook time: 15 minutes | Serves: 4

Nutrition per 4 servings: Calories: 911 | Carbs: 164 | Fibres: 12 g | Fat: 21 g | Protein: 24 g

Ingredients:

- ◇ Olive oil cooking spray (20 sprays)
- ◇ Salt to taste
- ◇ 2 Russet potatoes (cleaned and dried)
- ◇ 120 ml whole cow's milk
- ◇ 1 cup shiitake mushrooms (fried)
- ◇ 4 tbsps. full-fat sour cream
- ◇ Scallions, chives, or parsley (chopped, for serving)

Preparation:

1. Coat a baking dish with parchment paper or kitchen foil. Set aside. Heat the oven to Gas Mark 6, 375ºF, or 190ºC.

2. Cut the russet potatoes in half lengthwise. Coat the potatoes with a generous amount of cooking oil. Season to preference and place skin-side up on the tray.

3. Place tray in oven. Give the potatoes half an hour to roast. Remove potatoes from oven. Set aside to cool down for 5 minutes.

4. Coop the flesh of the potatoes out with a spoon. Add it to a bowl. Leave a margin of about half a centimetre of flesh onto the potato skins.

5. Pour the milk over the potato flesh in the bowl. Use a spatula to combine. Return the mixture into the potato skins.

6. In a small bowl, combine the sour cream and a splash of milk.

7. Top the potatoes with the fried shiitake mushrooms. Use the thinned sour cream to drizzle the potatoes and mushrooms. Top with desired garnish. Enjoy!

Prep Time: 10 minutes | Cook time: 0 minutes | Serves: 1

Nutrition per 1 serving: Calories: 311 | Carbs: 30 g | Fibres: 3.5 g | Fat: 15 g | Protein: 13 g

Ingredients:

◇ 1 package instant ramen

◇ 1 large free-range egg (fried or poached)

◇ 3 shiitake mushrooms (fried and sliced)

◇ 2 scallion springs (sliced)

◇ Salt and pepper to taste

Preparation:

1   Prepare the ramen as per package instructions. Transfer to a bowl.

2   Garnish with the fried egg, shiitake "bacon", and green onions. Season to taste. Enjoy!

Prep Time: 10 minutes | Cook time: 10 minutes | Serves: 1

Nutrition per 1 serving: Calories: 471 | Carbs: 33 g | Fibres: 6.9 g | Fat: 26 g | Protein: 31 g

Ingredients:

◇ 1 sliced finger roll

◇ 2 sliced tofu (100 g, fried)

◇ 1 cup shiitake mushrooms (fried, sliced)

◇ 2 slices swiss cheese

◇ Mustard of choice

◇ Pickled gherkins (finely sliced)

◇ 1 tsp. butter (melted)

Preparation:

1   Squeeze mustard on one half of the finger roll. Arrange the tofu slices over the mustard. Top with the fried shiitake mushrooms. Add the swiss cheese on top and finally the gherkins. Place the top finger bun on top.

2   Heat a griddle on low. Place the sandwich on the griddle. Use a silicon brush to coat the top bun with the melted butter.

3   Place a heavy pot on top of the sandwich to push it down. You can use a panini press if available. Cook for 5 minutes on low. Flip the sandwich, press it down again, and cook the other side for 5 minutes. Enjoy!

Prep Time: 15 minutes | Cook time: 30 minutes | Serves: 4

Nutrition per 1 serving: Calories: 1474 | Carbs: 110 g | Fibres: 20 g | Fat: 106 g | Protein: 29 g

Ingredients:

- ◊ 1 yellow onion (medium-large, chopped)
- ◊ 1 sweet potato (peeled, cubed)
- ◊ 1 garlic clove (minced)
- ◊ 1 can chickpeas (drained, rinsed)
- ◊ 2 tbsps. olive oil
- ◊ 150 g shiitake mushrooms (sliced)
- ◊ Vegetable stock as needed
- ◊ 28 g tomato puree
- ◊ 150 ml double cream

Seasonings:

- ◊ 1 tsp. ground cumin
- ◊ 1 tsp. ground coriander
- ◊ 1 tsp. turmeric powder
- ◊ 1 tsp. curry powder
- ◊ 1 tsp. paprika powder
- ◊ 1 tsp. cayenne pepper (optional)
- ◊ Fresh parsley (for serving)
- ◊ Chapati (optional, for serving)

Preparation:

1 Fry the onion in the olive oil on low heat until translucent. Add the minced garlic. Sauté until fragrant on low heat. Add the seasonings. Stir with a spatula until well combined.

2 Increase heat to moderate-high. Add the shiitake mushrooms. Sauté for 2 minutes. Grab the sweet potatoes and chickpeas and add them to the pan. Pour over 200 ml of stock and the tomato puree and mix. Give it 10 minutes to simmer with the lid on.

3 Remove the lid and add the heavy cream. Stir with a spatula to combine. Give the curry 15 more minutes to simmer. Check that the sweet potatoes are tender. Taste the curry and adjust seasonings to preference.

4 Serve the curry hot with chapati. Decorate with freshly chopped parsley!

Ingredients:

- ◊ 2 tbsps. butter
- ◊ 1 yellow onion (chopped)
- ◊ 10 cloves of garlic (organic, minced)
- ◊ 2 cauliflower heads (riced)
- ◊ Salt and pepper to taste
- ◊ 2 litres vegetable broth
- ◊ 400 ml water (less or more depending on desired thickness)
- ◊ 2 fresh thyme springs
- ◊ 75 g parmesan cheese (vegetarian, shaved or grated)
- ◊ Fresh chives (finely chopped, for serving)

RIAN CAULIFLOWER SOUP

Preparation:

1   In a pot that can accommodate all ingredients, heat butter and sauté the garlic and onion for 1-3 minutes over moderate-low heat. Season to preference and stir with a spatula to combine.

2   Add the cauliflower rice and stir. Pour the water and vegetable broth. Stir. Adjust heat to moderate and bring to a boil. Add the fresh thyme springs. Place a lid on the pan pot and allow the soup 15 minutes to simmer.

3   Remove lid from pot and remove the thyme springs from the soup. Blend the soup to desired smoothness with an immersion blender. Add the parmesan and stir to combine. Let the soup simmer for 2-3 more minutes.

4   Transfer to soup bowls. Serve hot with the chopped chives. Enjoy!

Tips!!! Add a russet potato to the soup to make it thicker. You can also add double cream instead of parmesan cheese. Season with favourite seasonings, including cayenne pepper, chilli, turmeric, etc.

Prep Time: 5 minutes | Cook time: 20 minutes | Serves: 2
Nutrition per 2 servings: Calories: 974 | Carbs: 125 | Fibres: 17 g | Fat: 39 g | Protein: 39 g

Ingredients:

- ◇ 2 tbsps. extra virgin olive oil
- ◇ Dried thyme to taste
- ◇ 3 garlic cloves (organic, minced
- ◇ Salt to taste
- ◇ 500 g chestnut mushrooms (sliced)
- ◇ 250 ml water
- ◇ 350 ml vegetable stock
- ◇ 170 g dried red and white quinoa
- ◇ Freshly chopped parsley (for serving)
- ◇ Cubed feta (for serving)
- ◇ 2 free range large eggs (poached, for serving, optional)

Preparation:

1. Sauté mushrooms with the thyme and salt in olive oil over moderate heat. Let cook for 5 minutes and stir in the garlic. Cook mushrooms for 8 more minutes. Set aside.

2. Meanwhile, in a medium pot, add the water and broth. Bring to a boil. Add in the quinoa, cover, and give it 15-20 minutes to cook through. All liquid should be fully absorbed by the quinoa. Remove from heat.

3. Stir the cooked mushrooms in the boiled quinoa. Add the freshly chopped parsley and stir until well combined. Transfer to serving bowls and garnish with cheese of choice and a poached egg for extra protein. Enjoy!

Ingredients:

- 2 tbsps. extra-virgin olive oil
- 5 garlic cloves (organic, minced)
- 2 carrots, cut into matchsticks
- 100 g snap pea
- 4 green onion springs (coarsely chopped)
- 2 tbsps. brown sugar
- 3 tbsps. soy sauce
- Salt and white pepper to taste
- 250g dry rice noodles (cooked)
- 1 green onion spring (finely chopped, for serving)

Preparation:

1 Set heat to moderate-low. Add green onions and garlic to a hot pan with the olive oil and sauté for 3 minutes.

2 Stir in the snap peas and matchstick carrots. Cook for 30 seconds. Pour the soy sauce and stir in the brown sugar.

3 Add the cooked noodles and stir gently to coat with the sauce. Cook for 2 more minutes. Season to taste and transfer to plates.

4 Garnish with the freshly chopped green onion and enjoy!

Tips!!! Add a touch of hotness with sriracha or cayenne pepper! Stir in finely sliced Chinese cabbage and matchstick bell peppers or sprinkle grated parmesan on top for an original touch!

Prep Time: 10 minutes | Cook time: 0 minutes | Serves: 2

Nutrition per 2 servings: Calories: 485 | Carbs: 22 g | Fibres: 14 g | Fat: 35 g | Protein: 28 g

Ingredients:

◊ 200g firm tofu (roasted, cubed)

◊ 50 g celery stalks (finely chopped)

◊ 30 g red onion (diced)

◊ Freshly chopped parsley

◊ Juice of 1 lime

◊ 1 ripe avocado (mashed)

◊ Salt and pepper to taste

◊ Crispbread or bread of choice (for serving)

Preparation:

1 Mash the avocado in a mortar with a pestle. Season to taste. Set aside!

2 In a bowl, add the diced tofu, chopped onions, celery, parsley, and mashed avocado. Mix to combine. Season to preference with lime juice. Taste and adjust seasoning.

3 Enjoy!

Tips!!! Substitute avocado with mayo for a more decadent version. Substitute avocado with Greek yogurt for a more refreshing version. Add pickled gherkins for a tangy touch!

Prep Time: 20 minutes | Cook time: 30 minutes | Serves: 2

Nutrition per 2 servings: Calories: 876 | Carbs: 164 g | Fibres: 30 g | Fat: 16 g | Protein: 30 g

Ingredients:

◇ 200 g brussels sprouts (quartered)

◇ 1 large red onion (peeled, wedged)

◇ Olive oil cookingspray

◇ 400 g sweet potatoes (diced)

◇ 1 can green lentils (drained and rinsed)

◇ Salt and pepper to taste

◇ 1 tbsp. maple syrup

◇ 3 tbsps. balsamic vinegar

◇ Salt and pepper to taste

Preparation:

1 Heat the oven to Gas Mark 7, 200ºC, or 400ºF.

2 Spread the sweet potatoes, onion wedges, and brussels sprouts on a baking sheet-lined oven dish. Spray with cooking spray. Season to taste. Mix to combine. Roast for 20-25 minutes. Remove the tray from oven. Transfer to a salad bowl.

3 Add the lentils to the roasted vegetables bowl. Mix the balsamic vinegar and maple syrup in a separate bowl. Add to the salad and mix well until combined. Taste and adjust seasoning accordingly!

4 Transfers to bowls and enjoy!

Prep Time: 30 minutes | Cook time: 30 minutes | Serves: 6

Nutrition per 1 serving: Calories: 1499 | Carbs: 181 g | Fibres: 27 g | Fat: 63 g | Protein: 54 g

Ingredients:

◇ 750 g white potatoes (peeled)

◇ 4 large free-range eggs (hardboiled)

◇ 3 large carrots

◇ 160 g peas (canned)

◇ 5-6 pickled gherkins (diced and drained)

◇ 3 tbsps. mayonnaise

◇ 2 tbsp. classic mustard

◇ 28 g pitted green olives

◇ Salt and pepper to taste

Preparation:

1. Boil the potatoes and carrots and remove from water. Set aside and let cool. Dice the pickled gherkins and place in a strainer to drain.

2. Dice the potatoes coarsely and cut the carrots in small cubes. Add to a large bowl. Cut the eggs into eighths and add to the bowl. Add the cooked garden peas and drained gherkins and give it a quick mix.

3. Add the mustard and mayonnaise to the bowl. Add progressively as some potatoes absorb quicker and more than others. Mix with a spatula for a homogenous texture. It should be sticky. Adjust seasonings to taste.

4. Transfer to bowls and enjoy with pitted green olives!

Prep Time: 15 minutes | Cook time: 20 minutes | Serves: 4-5

Nutrition per 4-5 servings: Calories: 2140 | Carbs: 186 g | Fibres: 29 g | Fat: 132 g | Protein: 77 g

Ingredients:

- 240 g wholegrain penne
- 150 g shiitake mushrooms (finely sliced)
- 2 tbsps. olive oil
- 300 ml single cream
- 50 g cheddar cheese (mature, grated)
- 50 g stilton cheese (crumbled)
- 20 g parmesan cheese (grated)
- Ground cumin to taste
- Garlic powder to taste
- Smoked paprika to taste
- Salt and pepper to taste
- Freshly chopped parsley (for serving)

Preparation:

1 Cook pasta as per package instructions. Drain and rinse. Set aside.

2 Meanwhile, heat the olive oil in a large work and stir in the sliced shiitake mushrooms. Sauté on moderate heat until cooked through.

3 Add the single cream and bring to a gentle boil. Reduce heat to low. Add the three cheeses and stir slowly until melted. Cook until the sauce thickens enough to stick to the back of a spoon or spatula. Taste and adjust seasonings accordingly.

4 Mix in the drained pasta. Stir until pasta are coated with the sauce. Plate the pasta and decorate with parsley.

Prep Time: 10 minutes | Cook time: 30 minutes | Serves: 2

Nutrition per 2 servings: Calories: 931 | Carbs: 151 g | Fibres: 32 g | Fat: 29 g | Protein: 27 g

Ingredients:

- ◈ 1 yellow onion
- ◈ 1 yellow or orange bell pepper
- ◈ 1 large carrot
- ◈ 2 tbsps. extra-virgin olive oil
- ◈ 1 can mixed beans
- ◈ 2 sweet potatoes
- ◈ 250 ml or more vegetable broth
- ◈ 56 g tomato puree concentrate
- ◈ Cayenne pepper to taste
- ◈ 1 bay leaf
- ◈ Salt and pepper to taste
- ◈ Freshly chopped parsley (for serving)
- ◈ Shaved parmesan (optional, for serving)

Preparation:

1   Peel and dice the onions. Set aside. Cut the carrot and bell pepper into matchsticks. Set aside. Peel and dice the sweet potatoes. Set aside. Drain and rinse the beans. Set aside.

2   Start sautéing the onions, carrots, and bell pepper in a large wok on moderate-low heat. Give the veggies 8 minutes, or more, to cook.

3   Add the tomato paste concentrate, sweet potatoes, vegetable broth, and bay leaf. Stir to combine. Cover and increase heat. Let simmer for 10 minutes.

4   Remove cover, add the mixed beans, and let cook for 10 more minutes. Add more vegetable broth if needed. Season to taste with cayenne pepper, salt, and pepper. Allow 1 more minute to cook.

5   Transfer to plates and garnish with freshly chopped parsley! Enjoy!

Prep Time: 5 minutes | Cook time: 20 minutes | Serves: 8

Nutrition per 8 servings: Calories: 3261 | Carbs: 393 g | Fibres: 15.9 g | Fat: 119 g | Protein: 144 g

Ingredients:

◊ 1 ¼ whole milk

◊ 450 g elbow macaroni (dry)

◊ 200 g mature cheddar cheese (grated)

◊ Salt and pepper to taste (optional)

Preparation:

1 Pour the milk in a large pot over moderate heat and bring to a boil. Add the elbow macaroni and let simmer for 10 minutes for the macaroni to cook through. Stir continuously while the macaroni cooks through.

2 Remove the pot from heat. Add the grated cheddar and continue to mix for the cheese to melt completely. Season with salt and pepper if needed.

3 Transfer to plates! Enjoy!

Prep Time: 10 minutes | Cook time: 20 minutes | Serves: 4

Nutrition per 4 servings: Calories: 1658 | Carbs: 123 g | Fibres: 47 g | Fat: 89 g | Protein: 120 g

Ingredients:

◇ 3 broccoli heads (florets only)

◇ 3 cloves garlic (minced)

◇ 180 g mature cheddar cheese (grated)

◇ Salt and pepper to taste

◇ 4 large free-range eggs (poached)

◇ Freshly chopped chives, spring onion, or parsley (for serving)

Preparation:

1 Heat oven to Gas Mark 6, 375ºF, or 190ºC.

2 Arrange the broccoli florets in an oven-proof rectangular dish. Mix the garlic with the cheddar. Add over the broccoli in an even layer. Season with salt and pepper.

3 Place the casserole dish in the oven and bake for 25 minutes. Remove from oven and transfer to plates. Top with a poached egg and serve with freshly chopped chives, parsley, or spring onions.

TOFU TERRYAKI FRIED RICE

Prep Time: 10 minutes | Cook time: 30 minutes | Serves: 5

Nutrition per 5 servings: Calories: 2122 | Carbs: 245 g | Fibres: 25 g | Fat: 78 g | Protein: 110 g

Ingredients:

◇ 400 g firm tofu (cubed)

◇ 240 ml teriyaki sauce

◇ 2 tsps. extra-virgin olive oil

◇ 1 small yellow onion (diced)

◇ 2 garlic cloves (minced)

◇ 1 medium carrot (diced)

◇ 150g broccoli florets

◇ 3 large, free-range eggs

◇ 650g brown rice (cooked)

◇ 1 tbsp. sesame oil

◇ 2 tbsps. soy sauce

◇ Pepper, to taste

◇ Freshly chopped chives

Preparation:

1. Place the tofu in teriyaki sauce and place in the fridge for an hour.
2. Add the tofu cubes to a wok on moderate heat. Allow the tofu to cook through. Remove from the wok and set aside.
3. Sauté the garlic, onions, and carrots in olive oil in a wok for 10 minutes. Stir in the broccoli florets and allow to cook 4-5 minutes. Move the veggies to one side of the wok.
4. In the cleared side of the work, pour the beaten eggs and scramble. Combine the scrambled eggs with the vegetables. Add the cooked rice, teriyaki tofu, sesame oil, soy sauce, and pepper. Mix gently. Give the rice 10 minutes to crisp up.
5. Transfer to plates and serve with freshly chopped chives!

Prep Time: 15 minutes | Cook time: 4 hours | Serves: 6

Nutrition per 1 serving: Calories: 491 | Carbs: 45.25 g | Fibres: 8 g | Fat: 31.5 g | Protein: 11.25 g

Ingredients:

◇ 6 large bell peppers (deseeded and stemmed, "lids" removed)

◇ 450 g brown rice (cooked)

◇ 1 can sweetcorn (drained, rinsed)

◇ ½ red onion (diced)

◇ 1 can black beans (drained, rinsed)

◇ Salt and pepper to preference

◇ 100 g tomatoes (finely chopped)

◇ 130 g passata

◇ 200 g mature cheddar cheese (grated, divided)

◇ 120 ml vegetable broth

Preparation:

1. Add the rice, sweetcorn, black beans, onions, salsa, and tomatoes to a bowl. Mix to combine. Season with salt and pepper to taste.

2. Use the mixture to fill each pepper halfway. Use half of the cheddar cheese to top the rice filling. Add remaining rice filling and top with the rest of the cheese.

3. In a slow cooker large enough to accommodate all 6 bell peppers, arrange them cut side up. Add the vegetable stock to the slow cooker and set the timer to 4 hours on high. For a crispier texture, check the peppers halfway.

4. Transfer to plates and enjoy!

Ingredients:

- ◊ 200g cherry tomatoes (halved)
- ◊ 200 g tagliatelle (cooked, al delte)
- ◊ 190 g red pesto
- ◊ Salt and pepper to taste
- ◊ Parmesan cheese (optional, for serving)

Preparation:

1. Heat oven to 400ºF, Gas Mark 6, or 200ºC.

2. Mix the cooked pasta, pesto and parmesan (optional) in a bowl. Season to taste. Transfer to a casserole dish and place in the oven. Give it 10 minutes to cook.

3. Remove from oven and transfer to plates. Serve with freshly chopped basil and grated parmesan! Enjoy!

ONE-TRAY RED PESTO TAGLIAT

Prep Time: 5 minutes | Cook time: 15 minutes | Serves: 5

Nutrition per 1 serving: Calories: 2318 | Carbs: 183 g | Fibres: 22 g | Fat: 146 g | Protein: 74 g

Ingredients:

◇ 400 g cooked penne
◇ 2 tbsps. olive oil
◇ 170 g artichoke hearts (drained)
◇ 150 g spinach
◇ 450 g full-fat soft cheese
◇ 500 ml whole milk
◇ 1 tsp. salt
◇ 1 tsp. pepper
◇ 1 tbsp. garlic powder
◇ Freshly chopped parsley (for serving)

Preparation:

1   Sauté the spinach in olive oil over moderate heat in a wok or deep pan. Cook the spinach until wilted. Add the artichoke hearts and cook for 1 minute.

2   Add the soft cheese to the pan/work and stir until very well combined. Season with garlic, salt, and pepper.

3   Pour the milk and stir until smooth. Add the cooked penne and stir until the sauce coats the pasta evenly. Transfer to plates and serve hot!

4   Garnish with freshly chopped parsley. Enjoy!

Prep Time: 10 minutes | Cook time: 20 minutes | Serves: 6

Nutrition per 1 serving: Calories: 377 | Carbs: 40 g | Fibres: 2 g | Fat: 21 g | Protein: 8 g

Ingredients:

- ◇ 2 tsps. extra virgin olive oil
- ◇ 400 g firm tofu (drained, 8 slices)
- ◇ 1 tsp. sesame oil
- ◇ 3 cups broccoli florets
- ◇ 3 tbsps. vegetable broth
- ◇ 2 garlic cloves (minced)
- ◇ 1 tsp. grated ginger
- ◇ ¼ cup soy sauce
- ◇ 2 tbsps. agave syrup
- ◇ 1 tbsp. rice vinegar
- ◇ 1 tbsp. corn-starch
- ◇ 1 tbsp. water
- ◇ 1 ½ tsp. sesame seeds (toasted)
- ◇ Sesame seeds (for serving)
- ◇ Cooked egg noodles (for serving)
- ◇ Sliced green onions, for serving
- ◇ Egg noodles

Preparation:

1. Add the tofu to shimmering olive oil in wok over moderate-low heat. Fry for 2-3 minutes on both sides. Transfer to a plate, cube, and set aside.

2. To the same wok, add the stock and broccoli florets. Cover and simmer for 5 minutes. Uncover and increase heat to moderate.

3. Add the ginger, garlic, ginger, and sesame oil. Stir and cook until softened. Add the agave syrup, soy sauce, and rice vinegar. Combine corn-starch and water until homogenous and add to pan. Stir and cook to desired thickness.

4. Add the fried tofu to the wok and stir in the sesame seeds. Stir until all ingredients are uniformly coated. Transfer to plates and serve next to egg noodles. Sprinkle toasted sesame seeds and chopped spring onions on top. Enjoy!

Prep Time: 10 minutes | Cook time: 20 minutes | Serves: 2

Nutrition per 2 servingss: Calories: 872 | Carbs: 133 g | Fibres: 14 g | Fat: 30 g | Protein: 23 g

Ingredients:

◈ 2 tbsps. extra-virgin olive oil

◈ 1 bell pepper (chopped into matchsticks)

◈ 1 yellow onion (small, julienned)

◈ 2 cloves garlic (minced)

◈ 300g shiitake mushrooms (julienned)

◈ 1 pack egg noodles

◈ 250 ml vegetable broth

◈ 1tsp. cumin powder

◈ 1 tsp. ground paprika powder

◈ Salt and pepper to taste

◈ Fresh chopped parsley

Preparation:

1   Sauté the onion, bell pepper, and garlic in the olive oil in a wok over moderate-low heat for 6-8 minutes. Add the cumin and stir to combine.

2   Add the shiitake mushrooms and sauté for 5-8 minutes. Add the egg noodles and vegetable broth and cover. Season with salt and pepper. Simmer for 5 or more minutes until the noodles are cooked through. Stir occasionally to combine.

3   Taste and adjust seasonings accordingly. Transfer to plates and enjoy chopped with freshly chopped parsley.

Being a vegetarian is a not about completing yet another diet. It is about discovering a lifestyle and new eating habits that will eventually contribute to a healthier version of you. Embracing this challenge is an amazing way to learn new food tricks, enjoy simple cooking, and plan your meals. Don't think of this challenge in terms of restrictions; think about it in terms of new foods, new flavours, new tastes, new ingredients! Don't forget the best part: you get to cook like a chef following simple instructions in the comfort of your own home!

Vegetarianism is surprisingly easy to adopt, and this challenge brings it to your home. Learn how you can make 3-5 varieties of the same Breakfast easy and quickly. You will soon discover the benefits. You will feel more energetic, your body will feel revigorated by eating clean, your sleep will improve, and your skin will glow. In addition, you will save lives and minimise your environmental impact. If you choose to go vegetarian for good, you will be able to reduce the risk of developing diabetes, cancer, or heart and kidney conditions! Start your challenge!

Breakfast: **Cheesy scrambled eggs**

Time: 5 minutes | Serves: 1
Net carbs: 13.6 g | Fibre: 1 g | Fat: 39.2 g | Protein: 27.5 g | Kcal: 531

Ingredients:

◇ 1 slice wholegrain bread (toasted)

◇ 1 tbsp. butter

◇ 2 eggs

◇ 50 g cheddar cheese

◇ Salt and pepper to taste

Preparation:

1 In a small bowl, crack the eggs and season with salt and pepper to taste. Beat them until the consistency is smooth and frothy. Set aside.

2 Heat the butter in a small-medium pan over moderate heat. When melted, spread uniformly on the pan. Pour the eggs and spread evenly, like an omelette.

3 Add an even layer of grated cheddar cheese on top. Reduce heat and start scrambling gently using a spatula. Egg should be cooked, but not over cooked. 2-3 minutes on low heat should be enough!

4 Transfer onto toast and enjoy!

Lunch: **Vegetarian jacket potatoes** *(page-26)*

Dinner: **Decadent three-cheese pasta** *(page-46)*

Breakfast: **Fluffy Breakfast omelette** *(page-12)*

Lunch: **Tzatziki and roasted chickpeas Greek-style pitas**

Time: 30 minutes | Serves: 2

Nutrition per serving: Carbs: 45 g | Fibre: 7.5 g | Fat: 12.6 g | Protein: 11.5 g | Kcal: 331

Ingredients:

- ◇ 1 tbsp. extra-virgin olive oil
- ◇ ¼ tsp. salt
- ◇ 1 tsp. ground black pepper
- ◇ 1 tbsp. ground paprika
- ◇ ½ tsp. cayenne pepper
- ◇ 1 can chickpeas (drained and rinsed)
- ◇ 250 g tzatziki

- ◇ ¼ red onion (sliced julienne-style)
- ◇ 2 lettuce leaves (coarsely chopped)
- ◇ 1 medium heirloom tomato (sliced)
- ◇ 4 soft pita flatbreads (microwaved for 30 seconds)

Preparation:

1 Heat oven to Gas Mark 6, 200°C, or 400°F.

2 Add chickpeas to a clean kitchen towel. Pat dry the beans to remove the skins. Transfer the chickpeas to a bowl. Add the seasonings: paprika, olive oil, black pepper, salt, and cayenne pepper. Toss to coat.

3 Transfer chickpeas to a baking sheet-coated oven tray. Spread evenly on the bottom. Roast the beans for 20-25 minutes. When done, they should be golden-brown.

4 Divide the veggies and chickpeas in four bunches. Spread ¼ of the tzatziki on one side of each pita flatbread. Top with the chickpeas, tomato slices, julienned onions, and lettuce leaves. Fold the flatbread and enjoy!

Dinner: **Protein-packed sweet potatoes stew** *(page-48)*

Breakfast: **Egg-wrapped vegetarian burrito** *(page-14)*

Lunch: **Vegetarian egg and shiitake ramen** *(page-28)*

Dinner: **Parmesan aubergine hassel back**

Time: 15 minutes | Serves: 2

Nutrition per serving: Carbs: 14 g | Fibre: 1 g | Fat: 15 g | Protein: 4 g | Kcal: 207

Ingredients:

- ◈ 250g marinara sauce
- ◈ 1 aubergine
- ◈ 1 Heirloom tomato (finely sliced)
- ◈ 125 g mozzarella cheese ball (sliced)
- ◈ Fresh basil (finely chopped)
- ◈ Salt and pepper to taste

- ◈ 2 garlic cloves (minced)
- ◈ Olive oil spray
- ◈ 2 tbsps. parmesan cheese (finely grated)
- ◈ 10 g panko breadcrumbs
- ◈ Salt and pepper to taste

Preparation:

1 Heat the oven to Gas Mark 5, 190°C, or 375°F.

2 Preparation: Holding the stem, usea sharp knife to slice the aubergine lengthwise. Keep the slices connected at the stem. Mix the parmesan cheese, panko breadcrumbs, and salt and pepper in a small bowl.

3 Pour the marinara sauce into the casserole dish and spread evenly. Add the aubergine on the sauce and spread like a flower to cover the bottom.

4 On each tomato slice, place alternately tomato slices, cheese, and basil. Season with salt and pepper, sprinkle with garlic, and spray with olive oil. Cover with kitchen foil and bake for 50 minutes. The aubergine should be tender.

5 Remove the dish from the oven. Uncover and top with the cheese and panko mixture. Return to oven uncovered and bake for 5 minutes.

6 Remove from the oven. Create portions as per preference. Enjoy!

Breakfast: **Coffee and chia pudding**

Time: 30 minutes | Serves: 2

Nutrition per serving: Net carbs: 12.6 g | Fibre: 7.6 g | Fat: 24 g | Protein: 5.9 g | Kcal: 282

Ingredients:

- ◇ 175 ml fresh coffee (cooled)
- ◇ 4 tbsps. chia seeds (heaped)
- ◇ 175 ml whole milk
- ◇ 2 tbsps. brown sugar
- ◇ 1 tsp. vanilla paste
- ◇ 1/2 tsp. cinnamon powder
- ◇ 1 tbsp. almond (nut of choice) butter
- ◇ Bowl or mason jar with lid

Preparation:

1. Mix all ingredients in a bowl until well-combined.
2. Place the lid on the bowl/mason jar and place in the fridge overnight.
3. Enjoy with freshly chopped banana slices or fruit of choice!

Lunch: **Cuban sandwich** *(page-29)*

Dinner: **Decadent mac'n'cheese** *(page-50)*

Breakfast: **Granola and berries Breakfast parfait** *(page-15)*

Lunch: **Fresh tomato and garlicky spaghetti**

Time: 15 minutes | Serves: 3

Nutrition per serving: Carbs: 90 g | Fibre: 5 g | Fat: 14 g | Protein: 24 g | Kcal: 631

Ingredients:

◇ 2 tbsps. extra-virgin olive oil

◇ 400g cherry tomato (halves)

◇ 3 garlic cloves (thoroughly minced)

◇ Salt and pepper to taste

◇ 230 vegetable stock or white wine

◇ 450 g spaghetti (dry)

◇ 110g parmesan cheese

◇ Freshly chopped tomatoes

Preparation:

1 Cook spaghetti as per package instructions. Reserve 250 ml of the water. Set aside.

2 Meanwhile, in a wok or large pan over moderate-low heat, add the tomatoes and garlic to the olive oil and season with salt and pepper. Stir to combine and reduce heat. Cook for 5 minutes on low heat.

3 When the tomatoes have released some juice, pour the wine. Give it 5-10 minutes to reduce. The sauce should become syrupy as the alcohol evaporates.

4 Add the pasta to the pan along with the 125 ml of the spaghetti water. Toss the pan to incorporate the pasta into the sauce and cook for 2 minutes for the pasta to absorb the flavours and cook completely.

5 Add the chopped basil (to taste) and the parmesan cheese. Toss the pan again to incorporate and add more pasta water if needed. Stir or toss gently until the parmesan is completely melted. The sauce should be smooth.

6 Transfer to plates and top with basil and parmesan cheese as per preference! Enjoy!

Dinner: **Cheesy broccoli casserole with sunny eggs** (page-51)

Breakfast: **Nutty banana oatmeal** *(page-16)*

Lunch: **Vegetarian cauliflower soup** *(page-33)*

Dinner: **Avocado and roasted chickpeas salad**

Time: 30 minutes | Serves: 6

Nutrition per serving: Net carbs: 29 g | Fibre: 12 g | Fat: 12 g | Protein: 13 g |Kcal: 326

Ingredients:

- ◇ 150 g mixed greens (arugula, swiss chard, baby spinach, kale, etc)
- ◇ 1 English cucumber (cubed to desired size)
- ◇ 300 g cherry tomatoes (halved)
- ◇ 1 avocado (California type, peeled, pitted, diced to bite-size)

Roasted chickpeas:

- ◇ 2 cans chickpeas (drained and rinsed)
- ◇ 2tbsps. olive oil
- ◇ 2 tsps. paprika powder
- ◇ 1 ½ cayenne pepper
- ◇ Salt and pepper to taste

Dressing:

- ◇ 2 tbsps. lemon juice (freshly squeezed)
- ◇ 2 tbsps. olive oil (extra-virgin)
- ◇ ½ tsp.each salt and pepper

Preparation:

1 Heat oven to Gas Mark 6, 200ºC, or 400ºF.

2 **Chickpeas:** Add the chickpeas to a clean kitchen towel. Pat dry the beans to remove the skins. Transfer the chickpeas to a bowl and stir in the seasonings: paprika, olive oil, black pepper, salt, and cayenne pepper. Toss to coat.

3 Transfer chickpeas to a baking sheet and spread evenly on the bottom. Roast the beans for 20-25 minutes. When done, they should be golden-brown.

4 **Salad:** Toss the salad ingredients (cucumber, mixed greens, avocado, tomatoes, roastedchickpeas) in a large bowl and toss to combine.

5 **Dressing:** In a small bowl, whisk the dressing ingredients into a smooth dressing sauce.

6 **Assembling:** Pour the dressing over the salad and toss to incorporate. Taste and adjust seasonings accordingly! Place in salad bowls and enjoy!

Breakfast: **Cheese-stuffed pancakes**

Time: 30 minutes | Serves: 12

Nutrition per serving: Carbs: 7 g | Fibre: 0 g | Fat: 2 g | Protein: g | Kcal: 61

Ingredients:

- ◇ 300 ml whole milk
- ◇ 2 large free-range eggs
- ◇ 100g plain flour
- ◇ 1 tbsp. vegetable oil
- ◇ 1 pinch of salt
- ◇ Cooking spray for frying
- ◇ Plain or chocolate-flavoured soft cheese (for serving)

Preparation:

1 Add all ingredients to a blender and blend to a smooth consistency.Set aside to rest for 30 minutes orcook immediately.

2 Spray cooking spray on a medium-sized crepe pan. Brush it uniformly on the bottom. Heat the pan on moderate heat.

3 In the hot pan, fry the pancakes for 1 min on both sides. They should be golden. Transfer to a plate and place in the warm oven until all batter is finished.

4 When done, spread soft cheese on top and roll. Enjoy with caster sugar on top!

Lunch: **Vegetarian cauliflower soup** *(page-33)*

Dinner: **Tofu teriyaki fried rice** *(page-52)*

Breakfast: **Gouda filled Breakfast omelette** *(page-17)*

Lunch: **Mushroom and guacamole Lunch wraps**

Time: 5 minutes | Serves: 1

Nutrition per serving: Carbs: 39 g | Fibre: 4 g | Fat: 18 g | Protein: 21 g | Kcal: 414

Ingredients:

◇ 1 whole wheat wrap

◇ 28 g full-fat soft cheese

◇ 1 tbsp. homemade guacamole

◇ 4 fried shiitake mushrooms (sliced)

◇ 2 lettuce leaves

◇ 100 g fried tofu cubes

Preparation:

1 Spread the soft cheese on the wrap. Top with the lettuce leaves. Arrange the mushrooms and tofu cubes in the centre. Place the guacamole on top. Roll and enjoy!

Dinner: **Slow-cooker stuffed bell peppers** *(page-54)*

Breakfast: **Hearty vegetarian Breakfast platter** *(page-18)*

Lunch: **Mushroom quinoa salad** *(page-35)*

Dinner: **Cheesy baked Marabel potatoes**

Time: 30-40 minutes | Serves: 4

Nutrition per 4 servings: Net carbs: 82 g | Fibre: 6.7 g | Fat: 80 g | Protein: 40 g | Kcal: 1216

Ingredients:

◇ 4 large Marabel potatoes (peeled, cubed)

◇ 230 g sour cream

◇ 100 g cheddar cheese (mature, coloured variety, grated)

◇ 2 garlic cloves (minced)

◇ Salt and pepper to taste

◇ Freshly choppedchives, spring onions, basil, or parsley

Preparation:

1 Heat oven to Gas Mark 6, 200ºC, or 400ºF.

2 Place the cubed potatoes in a large pot with salted water. Bring to a boil and let simmer for 10-15 minutes until the potatoes are par-boiled. Remove from pot and transfer to acasserole dish!

3 In a bowl, combine the grated cheddar cheese, sour cream, garlic, and saltand pepper. Pour over the potatoes in an even layer. Place in the oven and bake for 10-15 more minutes. Cheese should be golden, and the potatoes cooked through.

4 Transfer to plates and garnish with freshly chopped parsley or preferred greens. Serve next to avocado and lettuce salad drizzled in lemony vinaigrette!

Breakfast: **Zucchini wrapped Breakfast muffins**

Time: 5 minutes | Serves: 2
Net carbs: 3 g | Fibre: 1 g | Fat: 8 g | Protein: 1 g | Kcal: 82

Ingredients:

◇ 12-cup muffin tray

◇ 12 parchment paper muffin cups

◇ Cooking spray (for coating)

◇ 2 medium courgettes (sliced lengthwise with peeler)

◇ ½ cup feta cheese (crumbled)

◇ 6 large free-range eggs

◇ ½ cup whole milk

◇ Salt and pepper to taste

◇ 50 g courgette (finely diced)

◇ ⅓ cup mushrooms (finely diced)

◇ ⅓ cup tomato (finely diced)

Preparation:

1 Heat oven to Gas Mark 6, 200ºC, or 400ºF. Prepare the muffin tray by greasing it with non-stick cooking spray.

2 Remove the courgettes' ends. Peel the courgette into thin strips with a peeler. Use the courgette slices to line the muffin cups. They should stick to the cups.

3 Crack the eggs in a bowl and pour the milk in the same bowl. Beat the eggs and milk thoroughly and season with salt and pepper. Add the diced tomatoes, courgettes, and mushrooms to the mixture and mix to combine.

4 Place crumbled feta cheese on the bottom of the courgette lined muffin cups. Add equal amounts of the egg and veggie mixture to each cup. Place the tray in the oven and bake for 15-20 minutes. The edges of the muffins should be lightly browned.

5 Remove from oven and transfer to plates. Enjoy!

Lunch: **Garlicky vegetables wok noodles** *(page-37)*

Dinner: **One-tray red pesto tagliatelle** *(page-56)*

Breakfast: **Mozzarella, avocado, and egg toast** *(page-19)*

Lunch: **Heirloom tomatoes avocado and hummus toast**

Time: 5 minutes | Serves: 1

Nutrition per 2 slices: Net carbs: 31 g | Fibre: 19 g | Fat: 23 g | Protein: 18 g |Kcal: 462

Ingredients:

- ◇ 2 whole grain chia and muesli crispbreads
- ◇ ½ California-typeavocado (peeled, pitted, mashed)
- ◇ 2 tbsps. hummus (plain or flavour of choice)
- ◇ 4 slices Heirloom tomatoes
- ◇ 2 tbsps. toasted hemp seeds
- ◇ Cayenne pepper to taste (optional, for serving)
- ◇ Freshly chopped parsley (for serving)

Preparation:

1 Spread ½ of the hummus on each slice. Arrange half of the avocado slices on top of each slice. Place 2 heirloom tomato slices on top. Sprinkle the hemp seeds over the tomatoes and add a touch of spice with a little cayenne pepper.

2 Decorate with fresh parsley, finely chopped, and enjoy!

Dinner: **Cheesy artichoke and spinach penne** *(page-57)*

Breakfast: **Rich vegetarian Breakfast smoothie** *(page-20)*

Lunch: **Vegetarian "chicken" and avocado salad** *(page-39)*

Dinner: **Vegetarian red lentils soup**

Time: 30 minutes | Serves: 4

Nutrition for 1 serving: Carbs: 33.7 g | Fibre: 7.6 g | Fat: 4.1 g | Protein: 14 g | Kcal: 251

Ingredients:

- ◊ 1 tbsp.extra-virgin olive oil
- ◊ 1 large yellow onion (chopped coarsely)
- ◊ 1 tsp. ground cumin
- ◊ 2 carrots (medium, chopped coarsely)
- ◊ 200g red lentils (dried)
- ◊ 800ml vegetable broth or water
- ◊ 100 ml doublecream
- ◊ Salt and pepper to taste (ifneeded)
- ◊ Parsley (chopped, fresh, for serving)

Preparation:

1 Add the chopped onion to the hot oil in a pot over moderate heat. Add the ground cumin and stir to coat. Reduce heat and sauté for 2-3 minutes.

2 Add the dried lentils and carrots and toss to combine. Pour the veggiestock over the vegetables in the pot and give it a quick mix.

3 Increase heatto moderate and bring to a boil. Cover with a lid and reduce heat. Let simmer for 20-25 minutes or until the lentils and carrots are cookedthrough.

4 Remove pot from heat.Use an immersion blender toblendthe soup to a smooth consistency. Add the double cream and return to heat. Stir to combine and cook for 3 more minutes. Taste and adjust seasonings accordingly!

5 Transfer the soup to soup bowls and decorate with parsley!

6 ***Suggested toppings!!!*** *Grated cheddar cheese (or other hard or semi-hard cheese), finely chopped red onions (or chives, springs onions, cilantro), a dollop of soured cream (or crème fraiche, Greek yogurt), sliced avocados, diced jalapenos. For a decadent soup, add crushed tortilla chips!*

Time: 20 minutes | Serves: 3

Nutrition for 1 serving: Carbs: 54 g | Fibre: 11 g | Fat: 14 g | Protein: 13 g | Kcal: 377

Ingredients:

- ◇ 250 ml water
- ◇ 1 pinch of salt
- ◇ 200 g Arborio rice (dry)
- ◇ 1 tsp. vanilla extract

- ◇ 750 ml whole milk
- ◇ 120g sugar
- ◇ Cinnamon powder (for serving)

Preparation:

1. Place the water, a pinch of salt, vanilla extract and rice in a pot over moderate heat. Bring to a boil and let the rice absorb the water. Reduce heat to low.

2. Add the milk and stir to combine. Let simmer on low heat while stirring constantly until the rice is almost cooked through. Some rice is ready in 15 minutes. Other rice can take 20 minutes. Taste to check.

3. Stir in the sugar and continue to simmer for 5 more minutes or until therice has cooked completely. The milk should not be completely absorbed. Cover the pot with a lit and let sit for 5 minutes.

4. Transfer to serving bowls and let cool to set. The gluten in the rice should coagulate the milk and form a creamy pudding. Sprinkle with a touch ofground cinnamon! Heaven!

Lunch: **Roasted veggies and green lentils salad** *(page-40)*

Dinner: **Broccoli and tofu takeout-style** *(page-58)*

Breakfast: **Portable Breakfast jar** *(page-21)*

Lunch: **Tortilla chips Fattoush salad**

Time: 30 minutes | Serves: 6

Nutrition for 1 serving: Carbs: 17 g | Fibre: 4 g | Fat: 12 g | Protein: 3 g | Kcal: 202

Ingredients:

- 18 plain tortilla chips
- 2 cups quartered cherry tomatoes
- 2 cups diced cumbers
- ½ cup thinly sliced radishes
- 1 romaine lettuce head (chopped coarsely)
- 1 cup chopped parsley
- ½ cup chopped mint leaves (optional)

Fattoush Dressing

- 3 tbsps.freshly squeezed lemon juice
- ¼ cup extra-virgin olive oil
- ½ tbsp.white wine vinegar
- 2 garlic cloves (minced)
- 1tsp. ground sumac
- Salt and pepper to taste
- Feta cubes (optional, for serving)

Preparation:

1. **Dressing:** Add all ingredients to a bowl and mix until well combined.
2. **Salad:** Gently mixall salad ingredients in a large bowl. Pour the dressing over the salad and tossgently until allingredients are coatedwith the dressing.
3. Transfer to salad bowls and line the sides with the tortilla chips. Enjoy!
4. ***Tips!*** *Substitute the tortilla chips with home-made pita chips or oven-baked tortilla wraps!*

Dinner: **Shiitake noodles stir-fry** *(page-60)*

Breakfast: **Cheesy shiitake and spinach omelette** *(page-22)*

Lunch: **Oriental potatoes and egg salad** *(page-42)*

Dinner: **Spinach artichoke gratin**

Time: 50 minutes | Serves: 10

Nutrition for 1 serving: Carbs: Net carbs: 24 g | Fibre: 2 g | Fat: 13 g | Protein: 18.5 g | Kcal: 340

Ingredients:

◊ 225 g full-fat soft cheese(or cream cheese)

◊ 60 g parmesan cheese (finely grated)

◊ 150 g high-quality mozzarella cheese (grated)

◊ 25 g cooked spinach (chopped)

◊ 455 artichoke hearts (canned)

◊ 170 g full-fat soured cream

◊ 240 ml whole cow's milk

◊ 570 g vegetarian ravioli (frozen)

◊ Salt and pepper to taste (if needed)

Preparation:

1 Heat oven to Gas Mark 5, 190°C, or 375°F.

2 Mix the mozzarella, parmesan, and soft cheeses with the spinach and artichoke hearts in a bowl. Incorporate the soured cream and milk and mix to combine. Taste and seasonto taste accordingly!

3 Graba third of the artichoke mixture and spread in an even layer on the bottom of a casserole dish. Arrange ½ of the ravioli on the artichoke and cheese mixture. Repeat and top with the rest of the sauce.

4 Place in the oven and bake for 35 minutes or longer. The top layer should be lightly browned! Remove from oven and transfer to plates. Enjoy!

Breakfast: **High-protein Breakfast oatmeal**

Time: 15 minutes | Serves: 1

Nutrition for 1 serving: Carbs: 44 g | Fibre: 6 g | Fat: 3 g | Protein: 12 g | Kcal: 255

Ingredients:

◇ 1 ¼ cup whole milk (or plant-based milk)

◇ pinch of sea salt

◇ ½ banana (sliced)

◇ ½ cup rolled oats (high-quality)

◇ Cinnamon to taste (optional)

◇ Vanilla extract to taste (optional)

◇ ¼ cup cottage cheese

Preparation:

1 In a medium-sized pot, pour the milk and pinch of salt. Stir. Add the banana slices and oats and stir to combine. Turn heat tomoderate and bring to a gentle boil.Stir constantly and cook until liquid is fully absorbed.

2 Remove pot from heat. Add the cottage cheese and incorporate gently with a spatula. Taste and season accordingly with cinnamon and vanilla.

3 Transfer the oatmeal to a serving bowl. Serve as is or with preferred topping! Enjoy immediately!

4 Serving suggestion: top with almond slices, crushed pistachios, sliced banana, fresh berries, diced dates, nut butter of choice, or coconut flakes!

Lunch: **Vegetarian jacket potatoes** *(page-26)*

Dinner: **Decadent three-cheese pasta** *(page-46)*

Breakfast: **Fluffy Breakfast omelette** *(page-12)*

Lunch: **Vegetarian cobb salad**

Time: 25 minutes | Serves: 4

Nutrition for serving: Carbs: 8 g | Fibre: 9 g | Fat: 25 g | Protein: 46 g | Kcal: 475

Ingredients:

Vinaigrette:

- ⬥ ⅓ cup red wine vinegar
- ⬥ ½ cup olive oil (extra-virgin)
- ⬥ 1 tsp. maple syrup
- ⬥ 1 tbsp. Dijon mustard
- ⬥ Salt (cca ¾ tsp.)
- ⬥ Pepper (½ tsp.)

Salad Ingredients:

- ⬥ 4 large free-range eggs (hard-boiled, sliced)
- ⬥ 1 cup chestnut mushrooms (sliced, sautéed)
- ⬥ 6 slices firm tofu (grilled or fried, cubed)
- ⬥ 1 large cucumber (cubed)
- ⬥ ½ cup red onion (chopped)
- ⬥ 1 small romaine or cos lettuce head (chopped)
- ⬥ 1 cup plum baby tomatoes (halved)
- ⬥ ½ cup blue Stilton cheese (crumbled)
- ⬥ 2 avocados (pitted, peeled, sliced)

Preparation:

1. **Vinaigrette:** Add all dressing ingredients to a mason jar. Cover and shake the jar until well combined. Taste and adjust seasoning accordingly. Set aside.

2. **Salad:** Arrange a quarter of each salad ingredient Cobb-style on each of the four plates. Drizzle with the vinaigrette and serve immediately!

3. Serve with toasted sesame seeds!

Dinner: **Protein-packed sweet potatoes stew** *(page-48)*

Breakfast: **Egg wrapped vegetarian burrito** *(page-14)*

Lunch: **Vegetarian egg and shiitake ramen** *(page-28)*

Dinner: **Roasted cauliflower salad**

Time: 40-50 minutes | Serves: 6

Nutrition for serving: Carbs: 7 g | Fibre: 3 g | Fat: 8 g | Protein: 8 g | Kcal: 155

Ingredients:

Yogurt dressing:

◇ 140 g plain Greek yogurt

◇ 1 tbsp. extra-virgin olive oil

◇ 1 tsp. brown sugar or molasses

◇ 1 tbsp. Dijon mustard

◇ Juice of ½ lemon

◇ 1-2 garlic cloves (minced)

◇ 2-3 tbsps. dill (chopped)

For the salad:

◇ 2 tbsps. extra-virgin olive oil

◇ Florets from 1 cauliflower head

◇ Salt and pepper to taste

◇ ½ red onion (diced)

◇ 2 celery stalks (finely diced)

◇ 3 large, free-rang eggs (hardboiled, sliced or chopped)

Preparation:

1 Dressing: add all ingredients for the vinaigrette to a bowl or mason jar. Whisk to combine or cover the mason jar and shake to combine. Taste. Adjust seasoning accordingly. Set aside.

2 Heat oven to Gas Mark 6, 200ºC, or 400ºF. Coata sheet pan with parchment paper and arrange the cauliflower floretsevenly.Drizzle with olive oil and sprinkle with salt and pepper. Mix to combine.

3 Place the tray sheet pan in the oven. Allow the cauliflower about 25-30 minutes to roast, turning halfway. Leave the cauliflower 5-10 minutes longer for extra crispiness. Remove from oven and transfer to a plate to cool for 5 minutes.

4 Add all salad ingredients, including the dressing, to a large salad bowl. Use a spatula to coat the ingredients with the dressing. Plate the salad and serve immediately!

Breakfast: **Citrusy avocado Breakfast salad**

Time: 5 minutes | Serves: 2

Nutrition for serving: Carbs: 23 g | Fibre: 4 g | Fat: 24 g | Protein: 6 g | Kcal: 338

Ingredients:

- ½ large avocado, California type (pitted, peeled, sliced)
- 1 large grapefruit (peeled and cut into segments)
- 4 cups fresh corn salad (lamb's lettuce)
- 2 tbsps. walnuts (chopped)
- 2 tbsps. dried cranberries (unsweetened)
- 3 tbsps. creamy blue cheese (crumbled)
- Salt and pepper to taste (if needed)
- Balsamic dressing to taste

Preparation:

1. Place half of each ingredient in two salad bowls. Drizzle with balsamic dressing. Toss to combine. Taste and adjust seasoning accordingly. Enjoy!

Lunch: **Cuban sandwich** *(page-29)*

Dinner: **Decadent mac'n'cheese** *(page-50)*

Breakfast: **Granola and berries Breakfast parfait** *(page-15)*

Lunch: **Healthy eating new potato salad**

Time: 35 minutes | Serves: 4

Nutrition for serving: Carbs: 28 g | Fibre: 4 g | Fat: 8 g | Protein: 6 g | Kcal: 252

Ingredients:

- 600 g new potatoes (washed)
- 1 tbsp. salt
- ¼ cup shallots (peeled, finely diced)
- 2 cupsswiss chard (chopped)
- 4sun-dried tomatoes (finely diced)

Dressing

- 2 tbsps. extra-virgin olive oil
- 2 tsps. Dijon mustard (whole grain)
- ¼cup red wine vinegar
- 1 tsp. maple syrup
- 1 tbsp. shallots (minced)
- 1tsp. driedparsley
- Salt and pepper to taste
- 1 tsp. fresh chives (finely chopped, for serving)

Preparation:

1 Add the new potatoes to a pot and cover with cold water. Stir in the salt and bring to a boil over high heat. Reduce heat to moderate and let simmer for 20 minutes, or more, until potatoes are tender. Drain and let sit to cool completely.

2 Slice the potatoes into 1bite-size pieces. Add to a salad bowl along with the shallots, swiss chard, and sun-dried tomatoes.

3 Dressing: Add the ingredients for the dressing in a mason jar. Shake until fully combined. Drizzle over the potatoes bowl and toss until well coated.

4 Transfer to bowls and sprinkle with freshly chopped chives. Enjoy!

Dinner: **Cheesy broccoli casserole with sunny eggs** *(page-51)*

Breakfast: **Nutty banana oatmeal** *(page-16)*

Lunch: **Mushroom quinoa salad** *(page-35)*

Dinner: **Vegan lasagne soup**

Time: 30 minutes | Serves: 6
Nutrition for serving: Net carbs: 28 g | Fibre: 4 g | Fat: 9 g | Protein: 9 g | Kcal: 249

Ingredients:

- 9 shiitake mushrooms (fried)
- 3 cups vegetable broth
- 2 tbsps.maple syrup (optional)
- 1tbsp. extra-virgin olive oil
- 900 g sweet potatoes (peeled and cubed)
- ½yellow onion (finely diced)
- ¼ tsp. nutmeg
- ¼ tbsp. cinnamon
- ¼ tsp. cayenne pepper
- Salt and pepper to taste
- Freshly chopped chives (for serving)
- Crème fraiche (optional, for serving)
- Cinnamon (optional, for serving)

Preparation:

1. Heat the olive oil in a deep pan over moderate-low heat and sauté the onion until softened and translucent. Add the cubed sweet potatoes to the pan, along with the vegetable broth and seasonings. Cover the pan with a lid and bring to aboil.

2. Give the sweet potatoes circa 20 minutes to simmer until tender. When softened, add the maple syrup (optional) and stir gently to combine. Blend into a smooth cream using an immersion blender. Taste and adjust seasonings accordingly.

3. Transfer to soup bowls. Top with the fried shiitake mushrooms. Decorate with freshly chopped chives. For a decadent Dinner, add a dollop of crème fraiche or soured cream! Sprinkle with cinnamon! Enjoy hot!

Breakfast: **Vegetarian baked shakshuka**

Time: 20 minutes | Servings: 1

Nutrition per serving: Carbs: 16 g | Fibre: 8 g | Fat: 27 g | Protein: 21 g | Kcal: 412

Ingredients:

- ◇ 1 tbsp. olive oil
- ◇ 2 small red onions (finely diced)
- ◇ 1 garlic clove (minced)
- ◇ ½ tsp. salt
- ◇ ¼ tsp. red pepper flakes
- ◇ ¼ tsp. black pepper
- ◇ 300 g crushed tomatoes
- ◇ 2 large free-range eggs
- ◇ ¼ avocado (pitted, peeled, and finely sliced)
- ◇ 50 g cherry tomato (halved or quartered)
- ◇ Freshly chopped coriander (for serving)
- ◇ Crème fraiche (optional, for serving)
- ◇ Oven-safe pan/skillet (for cooking)

Preparation:

1 Heat oven to Gas Mark 4, 180°C, or 350°F.

2 Add olive oil to an oven-proof pan and heat over moderate-low heat. When hot, add half of the red onion, garlic, red pepper flakes, and salt and pepper. Sauté for 3 minutes until the garlic has become fragrant and the onion has softened.

3 Pour the crushed tomatoes on top of the seasoned onion and garlic. Stir to combine and let it come to a simmer. Crack eggs into sauce. Place pan in the hot oven and bake for 10-12 minutes or until the eggs are cooked to preference.

4 Remove from oven and transfer to plates. Top with tomatoes, avocados,onions, and freshly chopped coriander! Enjoy!

Lunch: **Garlicky vegetables wok noodles** *(page-37)*

Dinner: **Tofu teriyaki fried rice** *(page-52)*

Breakfast: **Gouda-filled Breakfast omelette** *(page-17)*

Lunch: **Healthy penne**

Time: 25 minutes | Serves: 6

Nutrition for serving: Carbs: 23.75 g | Fibre: 5 g | Fat: 5 g | Protein: 8.75 g | Kcal: 185

Ingredients:

- 225 dry penne pasta (cooked to instructions)
- 2 cups cucumbers (chopped)
- 2 cups cherry tomatoes (chopped)
- 1 cup red onion (chopped)

Dressing:

- 2 tbsps. olive oil
- 3 tbsps. balsamic vinegar
- ¼ tsp. red pepper (crushed)
- 1 ½ tsps. salt
- 2 tbsps. fresh basil (minced)

Preparation:

1. In a large bowl, combine the pasta with the choppedonion, cucumber, and cherry tomatoes.
2. In a mason jar, add the dressing ingredients and cover. Shake until well mixed.Add the dressing to the salad bowl and toss tocombine.
3. Place in the fridge and serve cold! Enjoy!

Dinner: **Slow-cooked stuffed bell peppers** *(page-54)*

Breakfast: **Hearty vegetarian Breakfast platter** *(page-18)*

Lunch: **Garlicky vegetables wok noodles** *(page-37)*

Dinner: **Sweet'n'sour tempeh**

Time: 30 minutes | Serves: 4

Nutrition for serving: Carbs: 48 g | Fibre: 5 g | Fat: 6 g | Protein: 14 g | Calories: 300

Ingredients:

- 1 tbsp. olive oil
- 2 orange bell peppers (chopped)
- 1 small red onion (chopped)
- 2 tbsps. cornstarch + 2 tbsps. water
- 450 g pineapple chunks (frozen)
- 225 tempeh (chopped)
- Quinoa (for serving)

Marinade Sauce:

- ½ cup water
- ¼ cup tomato sauce
- 2 tbsps apple cider vinegar
- 2 tbsps. tamari
- 3 tbsps. brown sugar
- 1 tsp. fresh ginger (grated)
- 2 garlic cloves (minced)

Preparation:

1 Add all sauce ingredients to a bowl with lid. Whisk the ingredients until well mixed. Add the tempeh and place in the fridge tomarinate overnight.

2 Heat olive oil in a large pan over moderate-low heat. Add the bell peppers and onions and sauté for 8 minutes. Add pineapple chunks and tempeh along with the marinade sauce. Stir to combine. Lower heat and simmer for 15 minutes.

3 Combinethe water withcorn-starch in a small bowl.Add to the pan and stirto combine. The sauce should start to thicken in less than 30 seconds. Remove from heat and transfer toplated brown rice.

4 Enjoy!

Breakfast: **Avocado and roasted leftover veggie salad**

Time: 20 minutes | Serves: 1

Nutrition for 1 serving: Net carbs: 9 g | Fibre: 7 g | Fat: 29 g | Protein: 17 g | Kcal: 370

Ingredients:

◇ 3 tsps. avocado or olive oil

◇ ¼ cup red onion (chopped)

◇ 2 cups spinach(chopped)

◇ 3 large free-range eggs

◇ ½ avocado (peeled, pitted, sliced)

◇ ½ cup roasted cauliflower (chopped)

◇ Fresh dill to taste (chopped, for serving)

◇ Salt and pepper to taste

Preparation:

1 In a large pan, sauté the onion in the avocado oil over moderate-low heat for 5 minutes.Add the spinach and cauliflower and give it a quick stir. Season to taste and cook for 2 minutes while stirringconsistently. Transfer to a bowl.

2 In the same pan, cook the eggs to preference. Add more oil if needed. Season with salt and pepper and transfer to the same bowl on top of the vegetables.

3 Garnish with the avocado slices and freshly chopped dill. Serve immediately! Enjoy!

Lunch: **Vegetarian "chicken" and avocado salad** *(page-39)*

Dinner: **Slow-cooked stuffed bell peppers** *(page-54)*

Breakfast: **Mozzarella, avocado, and egg toast** *(page-19)*

Lunch: **Lemony feta asparagus salad**

Time: 15 minutes | Serves: 4

Nutrition for serving: Carbs: 8 g | Fibre: 5 g | Fat: 12 g | Protein: 5 g | Kcal: 175

Ingredients:

- 900g fresh asparagus spears
- 1 cup red onion (chopped)
- ¼ cup feta cheese (crumbled)
- ¼ cup fresh parsley (chopped)

Lemony dressing:

- 3 tbsps. extra virgin olive oil
- Juice from ½ lemon
- 1 tbsp. Dijon mustard
- 1 tsp. maple syrup
- 1 garlic clove (minced)
- ½ tsp. salt and pepper each
- 2 tbsps. feta cheese (crumbled)
- Bowl of iced water
- Paper-towelled plate

Preparation:

1 Trim the ends of the asparagus spears and cut into thirds diagonally. Add to a pot of boiling water and give the asparagus 2 minutes to blanch. Drain and add to a bowl of iced water. Let chill for 2 minutes and transfer to a paper-towelled plate.

2 While the asparagus dries, prepare the dressing by mixing all ingredients in a mason jar. Shake until well combined.

3 Add the asparagus to a salad bowl. Add the parsley, red onion, and dressing as well. Mix to combine. Top with the feta cheese! Enjoy!

Dinner: **One-tray red pesto tagliatelle** *(page-56)*

Breakfast: **Rich vegetarian Breakfast smoothie** *(page-20)*

Lunch: **Roasted veggies and green lentils salad** *(page-40)*

Dinner: **Garlicky thyme roasted potatoes**

Time: 20 minutes | Serves: 5

Nutrition per serving: Carbs: 45 g | Fibre: 4 g | Fat: 10 g | Protein: 4 g | Kcal: 293

Ingredients:

◇ 12 new russet potatoes (washed, cut into bite-size pieces)

◇ 1 tsp. baking soda

◇ 1 tsp. salt

Herb infusion:

◇ 60 ml olive oil (extra virgin)

◇ 2 tbsps. garlic (minced)

◇ 2 tbsps. fresh thyme (finely chopped)

◇ Salt and pepper to taste

◇ Fresh parsley (minced, for serving)

Serving suggestions:

◇ sunny eggs and greens of choice salad!

Preparation:

1 Boil the potatoes along with the salt and baking soda for10minutesin a large pot over high heat. Potatoes should be fork-tender. Drain and return to pot to sit for 2-3 minutes.

2 Meanwhile, in a saucepan, add all the thyme/olive infusion ingredients and cook over moderate heat for 2-3 minutes. Stir constantly.

3 Pour the mixture over the potatoes in the pot. Season with more salt and pepper anduse a spatulato mix well until potatoes are coated uniformly with the thyme/olive oil mixture. Give the pot a good couple of shakes.

4 Heat oven to Gas Mark 7, 220ºC, or 425ºF. Line a large casserole dish with baking sheet. Add the potatoes to the dish arranging them in an even layer on the bottom. Transfer to oven.

5 Give the tatties 25 minutes to roast without moving. Flip them with a spatula and allow 25 more minutes to finish roasting. Shake the potatoes to break them 3-4 times during the last stage of roasting. They should be nice and crispy at the end.

6 Transfer to a bowl and season with the minced parsley and more salt and pepper if needed. Plate the potatoes and serve hot with sunny eggs and greens salad!

Breakfast: **Two-ways Breakfast muffins**

Time: 30 minutes | Serves: 12

Nutrition per serving: Net carbs: 30 g | Fibre: 6.6 g | Fat: 17.5 g | Protein: 8.33 g | Kcal: 232

Ingredients:

◇ 9 ripe bananas

◇ 150 g blueberry

◇ 60 g cocoa powder

◇ 360 g nut butter of choice

Preparation:

1 Heat the oven to 180°C (350°F).

2 Use a fork to mash the bananas. Mix in the nut butter until well combined. Place ½ of the batter into one bowl and the remaining half into a separate bowl.

3 **Cocoa muffins:** Incorporate the cocoa powder into the first bowl.

4 **Blueberry muffins:** Incorporate the blueberries into the second bowl.

5 Pour the cocoa batter into 6 cups of the muffin tin. Pour the blueberry batter into 6 cups of the muffin tin. Transfer to muffins and bake for 20 minutes. Let muffins cool.

Lunch: **Oriental potatoes and egg salad** *(page-42)*

Dinner: **Cheesy artichoke and spinach penne** *(page-57)*

Printed in Poland
by Amazon Fulfillment
Poland Sp. z o.o., Wrocław